Don't Touch Me

"I said No!"

A story all adults should read to children

I dedicate this book to all children
And my grandchildren Kwabena-Kaylum and A'laiyah

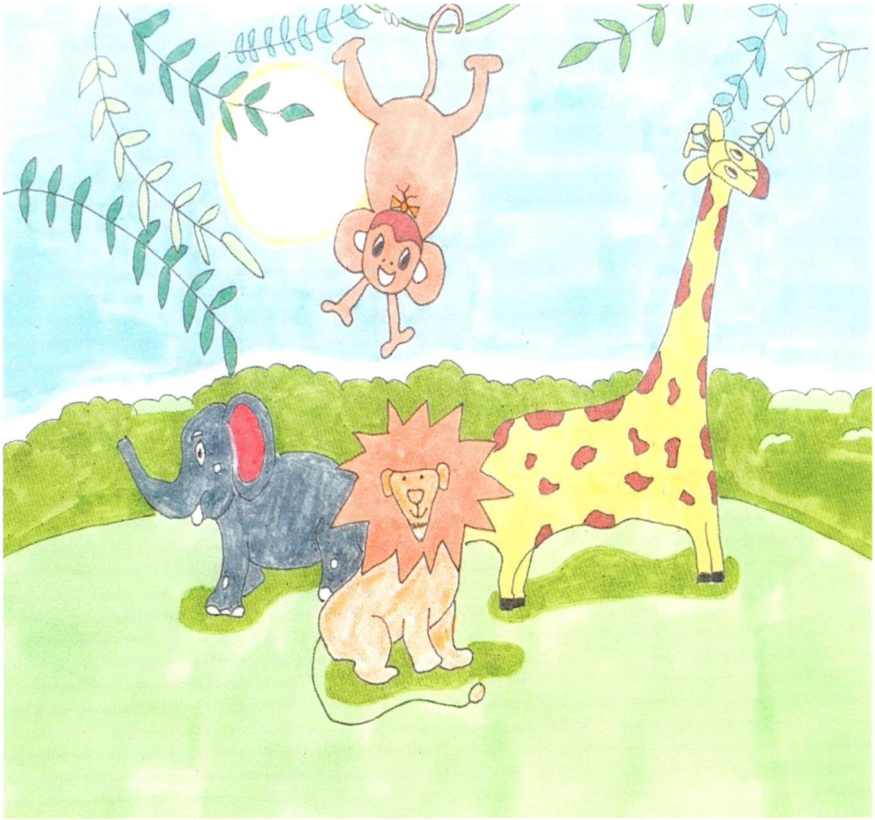

Once upon a time there were these animals that lived in Africa, a very hot country. They were happy and loved being in their country.

Their names were Kwame - the Giraffe; Aba - the Monkey; Asha - the Elephant, and Ade - the Lion.

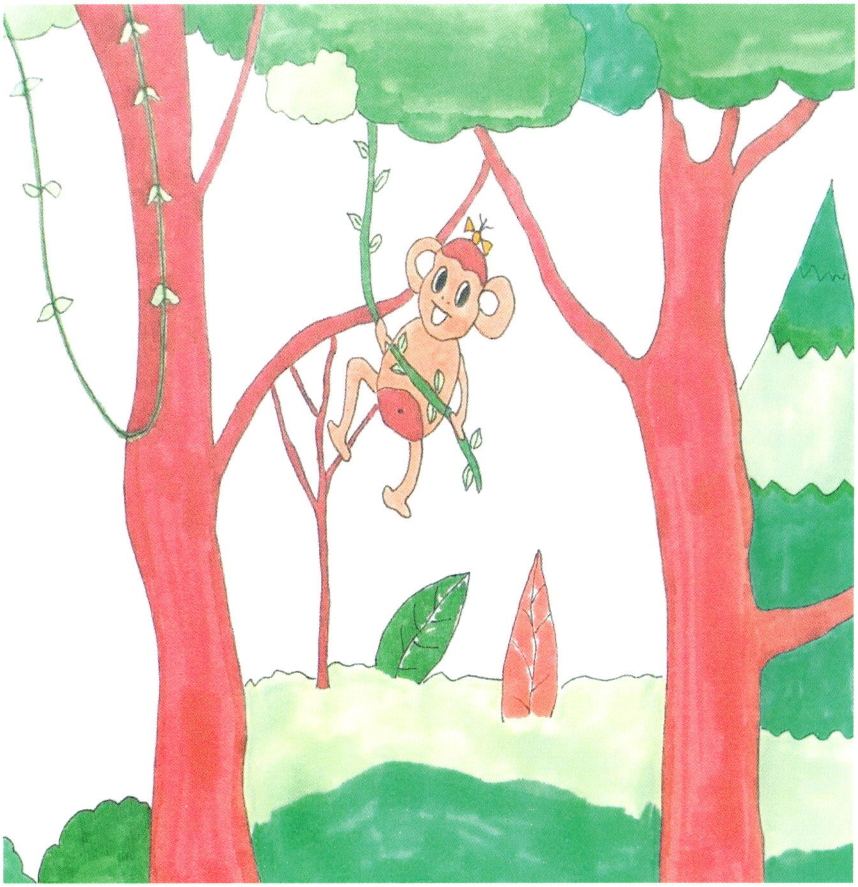

One day, Aba the Monkey received a message from another animal Fumi the Zebra that there were children in another country, called England, who needed their help.

Aba swung through the trees to where her friends were gathered by the lake, to give them the message.

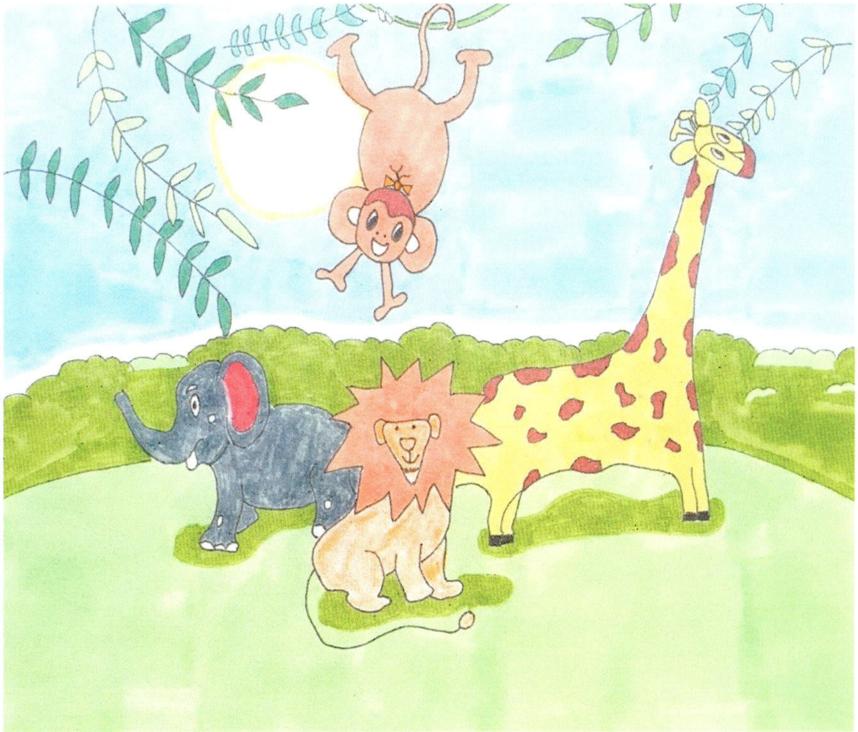

At the lake, Aba the Monkey, called all her friends around and said, "Listen everyone, we've a problem. There are children in another country that need our help."

"Here we go again," said Kwame the Giraffe, "You always come to us to try and save the world."

"I know but this time, the problem is very serious," Aba grunted.

Swinging her trunk, Asha the Elephant walked over and said, "Ok tell us all about it, with our gifts we should be able to help to make a difference."

Each animal was special since they all had their own gift that none of them took for granted.

Kwame the Giraffe, not only could see very far because of his long neck, he also had the ability to speak to people's minds. Ade the Lion, had a loud roar and speed that made him quick as lightening. Asha the Elephant, was big and strong, and had the wisdom to heal anyone's soul. While being able to swing through trees, Aba the Monkey, could also see into the future.

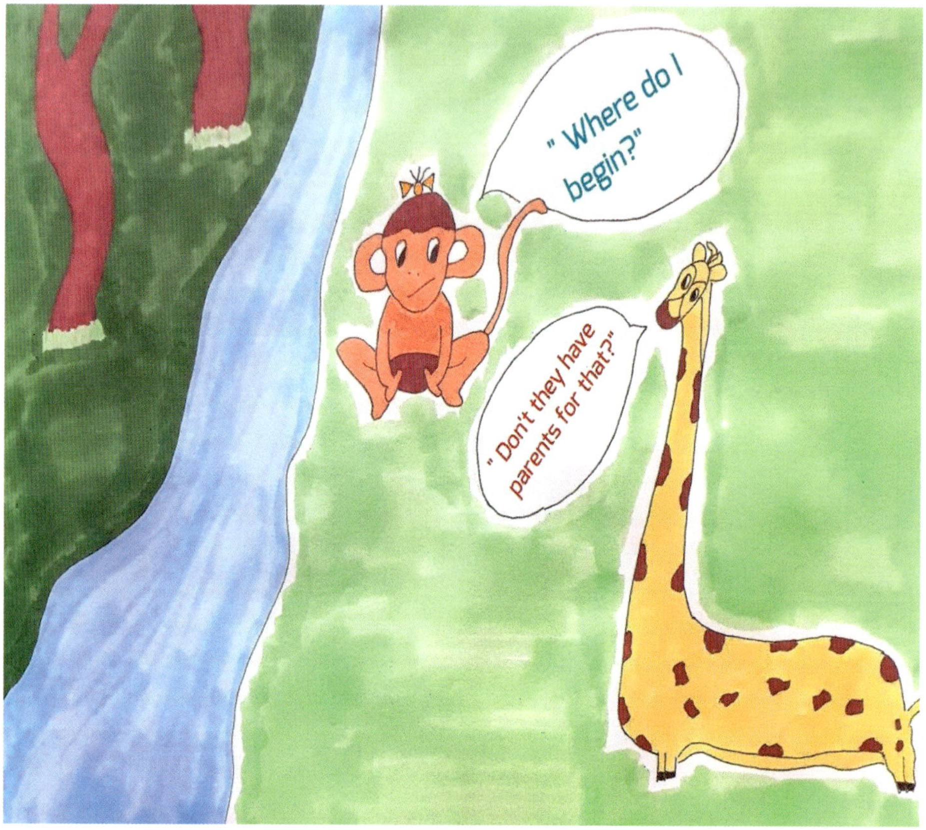
" Where do I begin?"
" Don't they have parents for that?"

"Where do I begin?" asked Aba the Monkey. "There are children who need our help on safety and protecting their own bodies."

"Don't they have parents for that?" said Ade.

"Yes they do," answered Aba, "but it's not enough, the world is changing so fast they can't keep up."

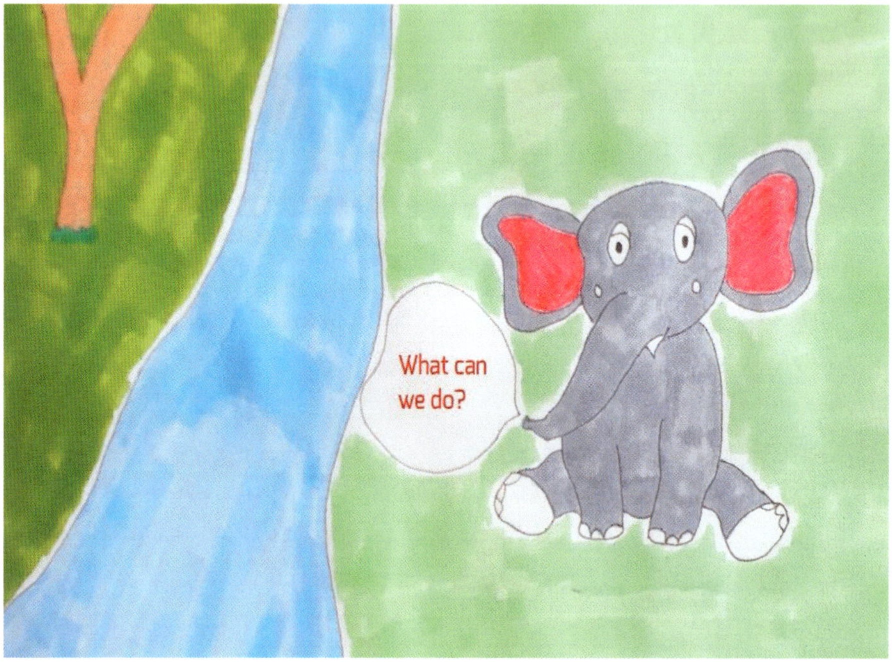
What can we do?

"Ok, so what can we do?" Asha the Elephant asked. "We're only animals why should they listen to us?"

"Because we have the experience and the knowledge to share what we know, our powers will help us."

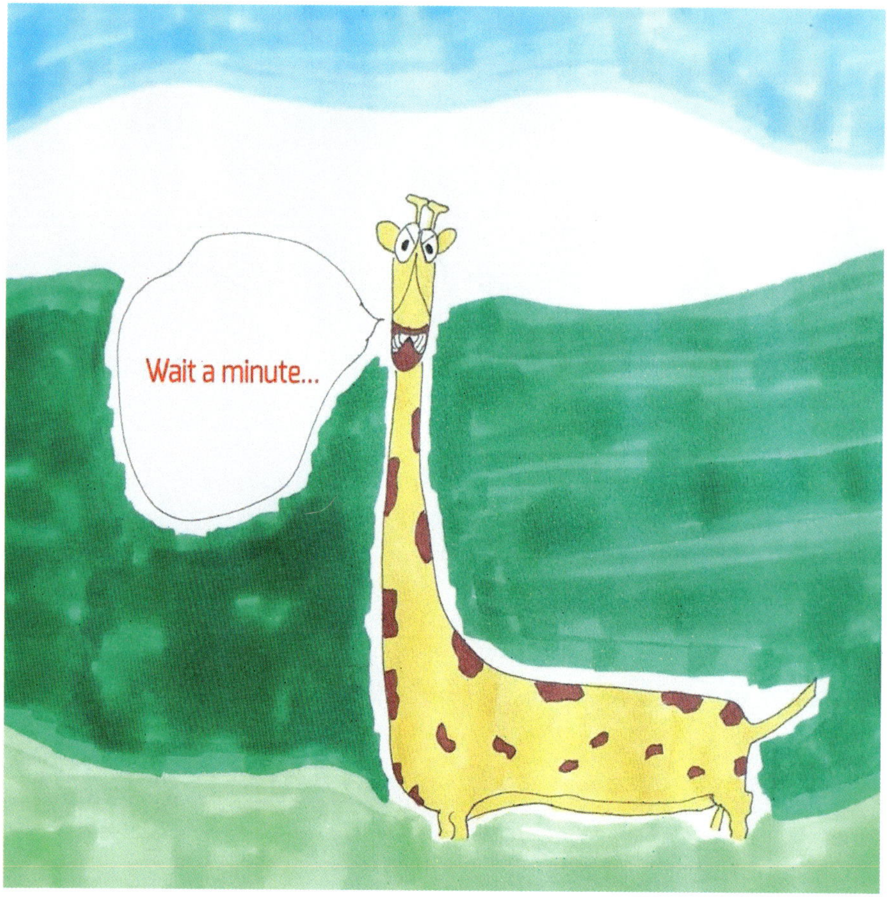
Wait a minute...

"So where are these children?" asked Asha, shaking her big trunk. In England stated Aba the Monkey.

"Wait a minute...you mean to tell me we're not just trying to help these children but have to travel to their cold country too?" said Kwame.

"It'll be fun, like an adventure," laughed Aba. "Come on guys, these children really need our help."

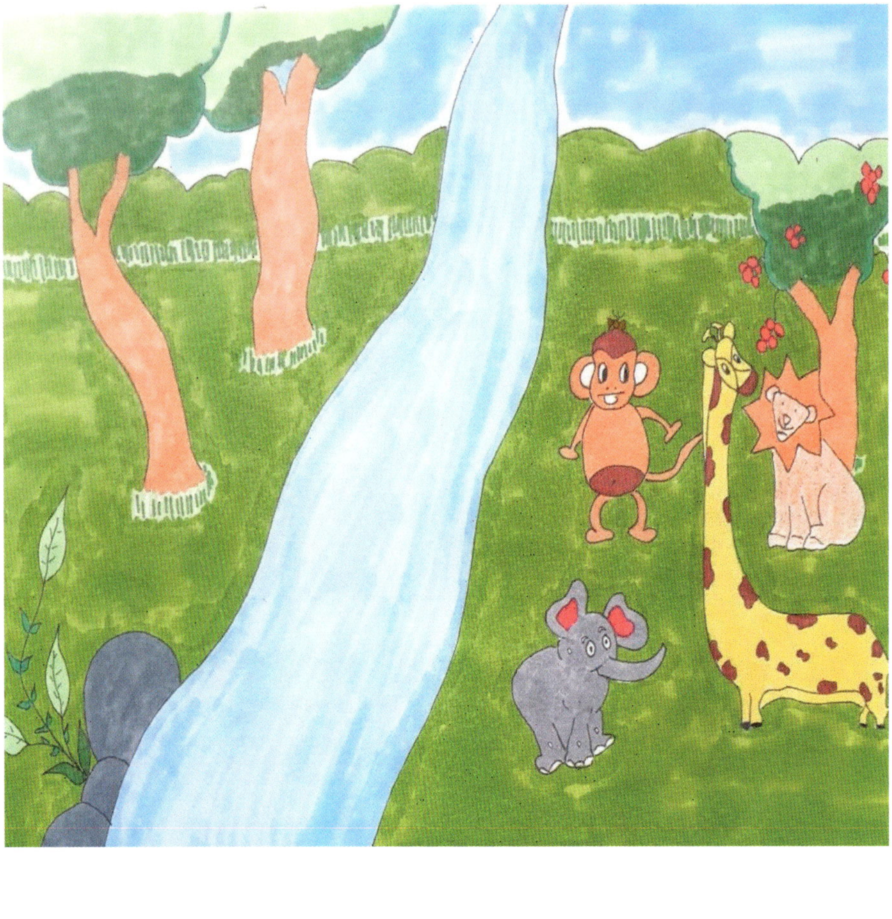

The friends looked at each other before nodding in agreement. Kwame the Giraffe said, "You know, I remember what it was like before you guys took me in as family. I was alone and had no awareness or idea of how to protect my body."

"I felt that I had no purpose in life but you all showed me love and gave me hope, so I can see how we can help in some way."

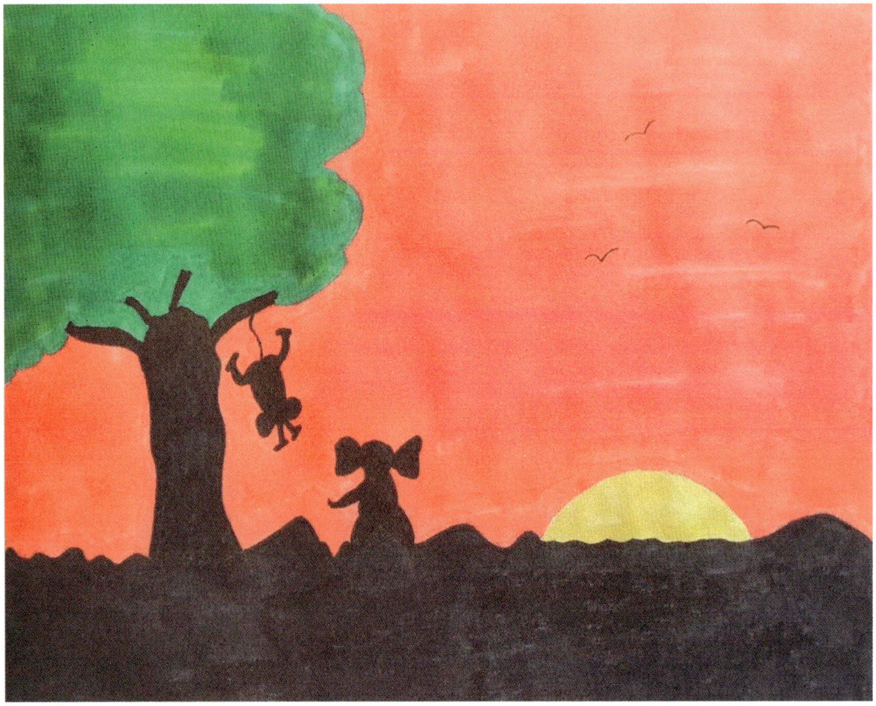

The sun was going down and by the evening the animals tried to work out how it was going to work how long it would take for them to travel, what could happen when they got to England and how would they communicate with the people there.

Asha, the Elephant asked, "So now that we know we are doing this and we know we want to help, when do we leave?"

"No time like the present," confirmed Aba the Monkey.

"WHAT!" said Kwame. "You mean tonight?"

"No silly," said Aba, chuckling. They all laughed. They could not wait for tomorrow.

Leaving the lake behind, they each went to their separate homes.

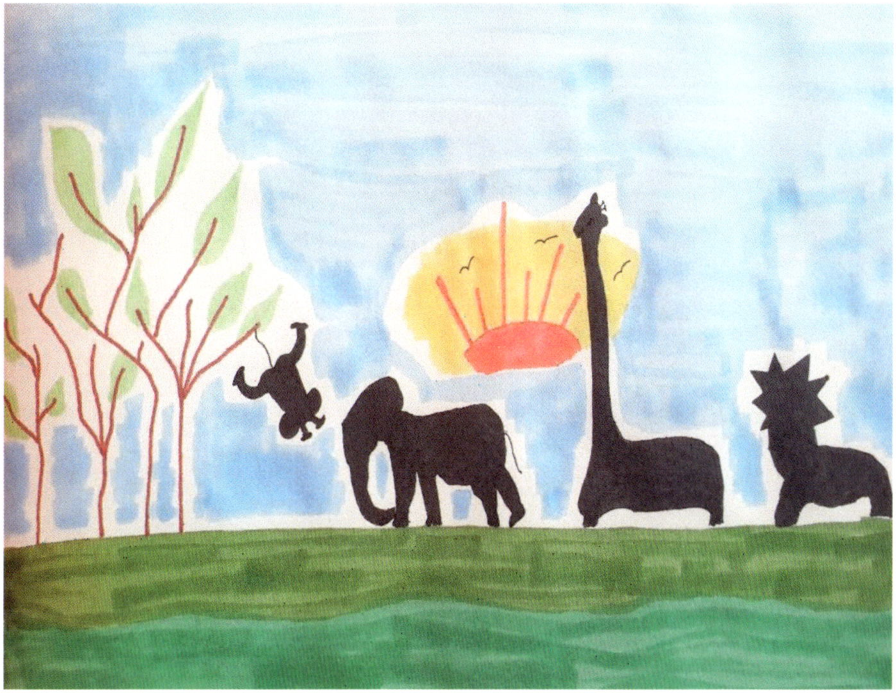

Morning came and the animals got ready to set off on their long journey to England. Kwame was not looking forward to being in a cold country where there was snow, rain and cold wind.

They travelled, walking for many months, finding food along the way. Finally, they reached England. It was wet and cold.

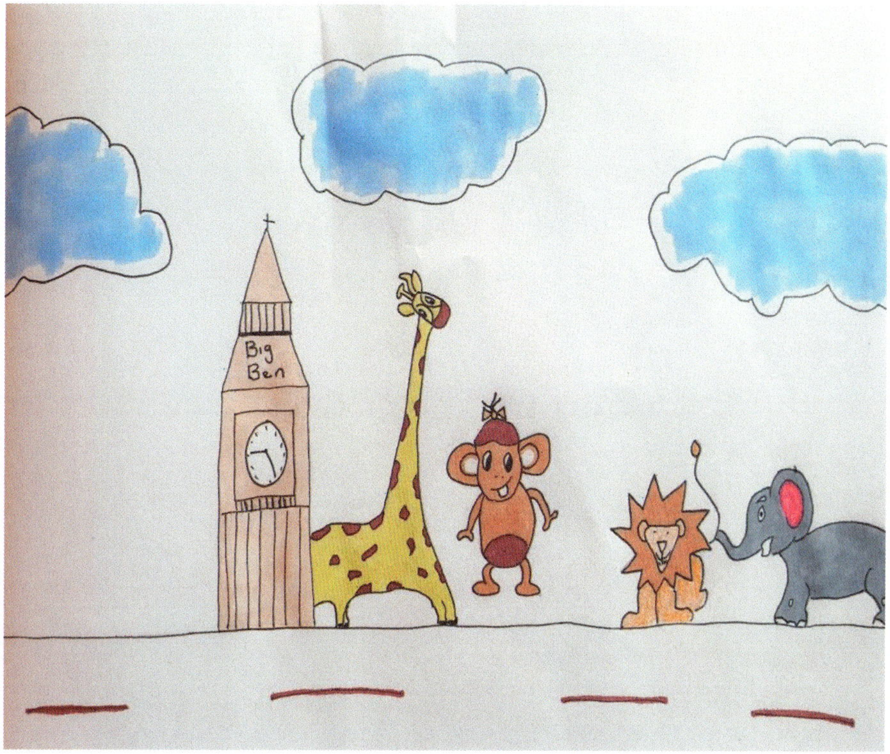
Big Ben

"Ok, now that we have arrived, here's the plan," said Aba the Monkey. Aba was the organiser and who always came up with the plans. "I already know what children we are going to speak with since there are four of us and four of them. We will each have one child."

"But I thought we were saving all children?" asked Ade the Lion.

"By talking to just a few children, they will pass on the message to the others and that's how it will get around to all the children around the world," answered Aba. "Don't worry this will work."

Aba explained to the others what needed to be done and gave them all the information on how to speak to the children and get the message across.

Excited, the animals thought this may not be so bad after all and even Kwame had a little smile on his long face even though he was feeling the cold.

Nodding, they understood what needed to be done and headed off to start their missions.

The Game Kiss Chase: Children running after another to kiss them

Mission: Kwame the Giraffe
Young person: 6-year-old Alice

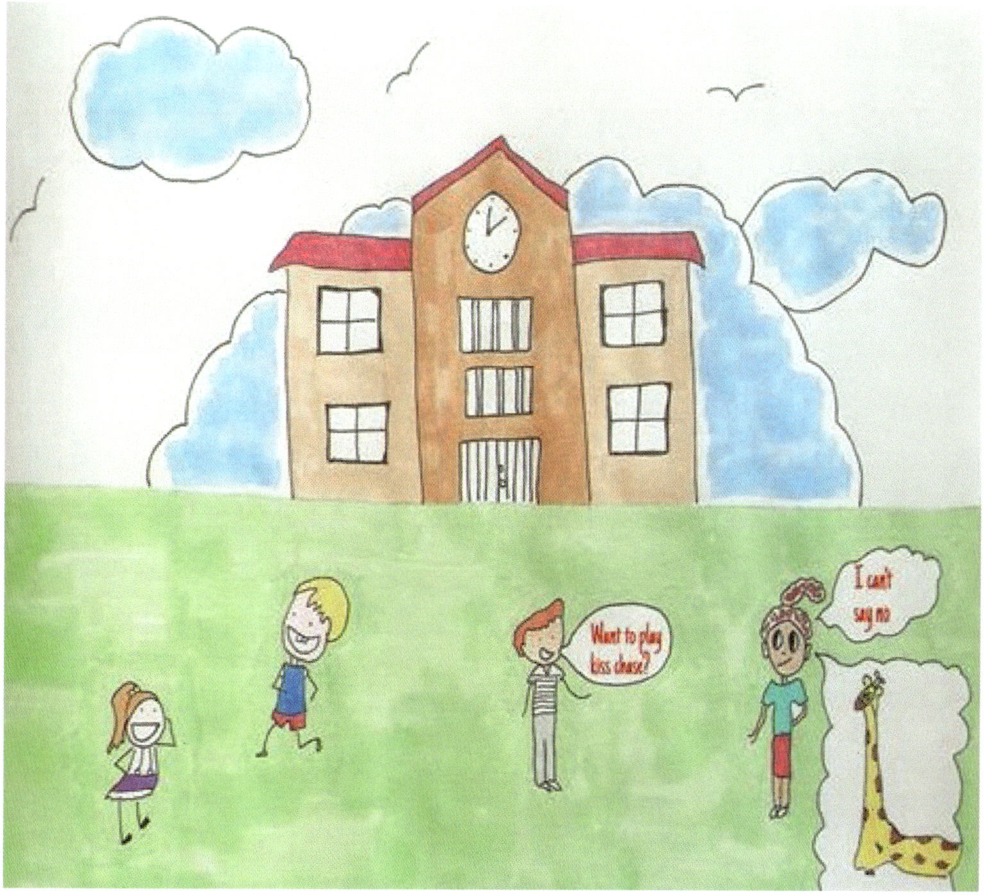
Want to play kiss chase?
I cant say no

Alice was in her school playground and a couple of her friends were playing the Kiss Chase game. They asked Alice if she wished to play. Alice did not want to but could not say no.

Kwame stepped in. "Kiss Chase is not a children's game Alice," he said.

"Wow," said Alice. "I just heard a voice in my head."

"You're right," said Kwame. "Go and tell them no, Kiss Chase is not a children's game and then go and tell your teacher". "When you say the magic words *I said no*, you'll have the powers to change the game."

"Wow," said Alice. "Thank you so much. I now have the powers to say no and make up another game."

Joyful, Alice ran off to tell her friends, shouting as she went: "I said no that game isn't a children's game but I do have another game we can play. It's called Shops."

Smiling, Kwame was chuffed. He felt proud, he had completed his mission.

The Game Mums & Dads: children playing a mum and a dad, adult roles

Mission: Ade the Lion,
Young person: 8-year-old David

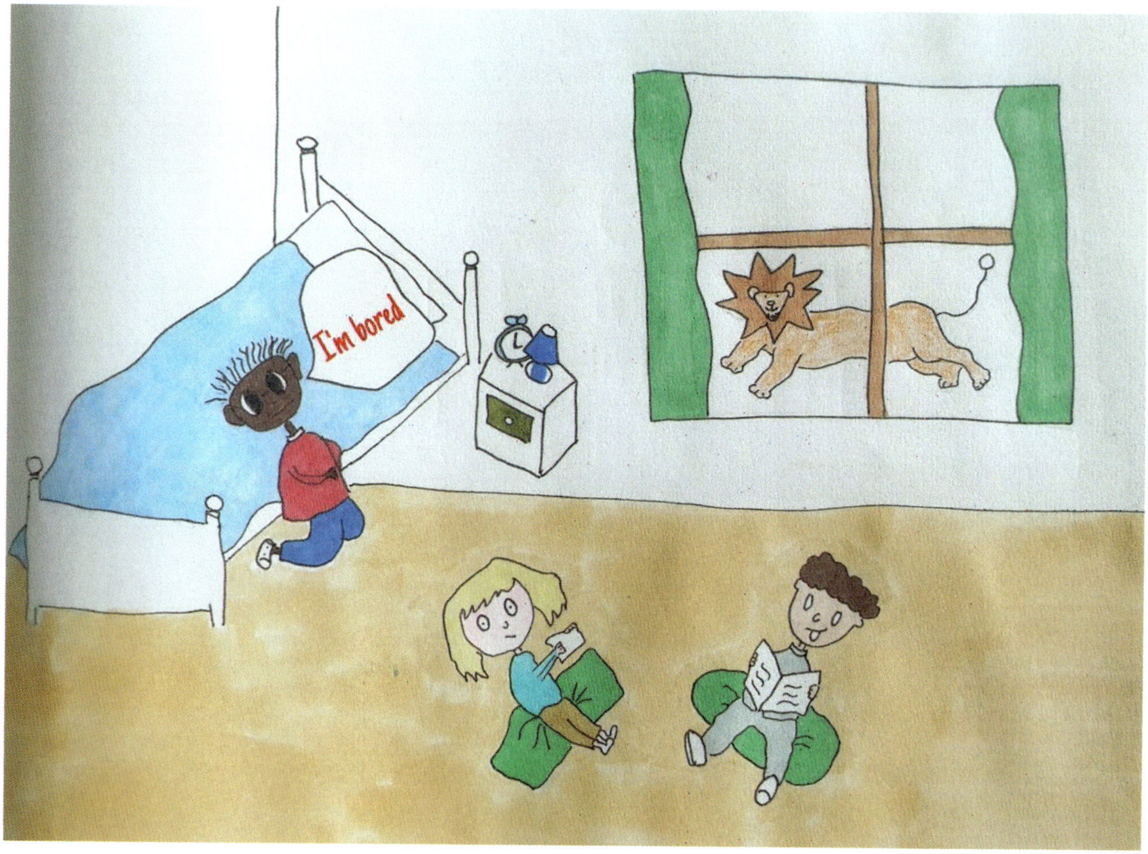
I'm bored

David is at his friend's house playing in their room, they are bored so David said, "I know of a game let's play Mums and Dads."

Ade the Lion, sped pass David's window.

David glimpsed him and said, "Hold on a minute! What is that outside?" and ran outside to see.

He came across a lion on the road. "Oh my, where have you come from?"

Ade purred. "I'm here to give you a message."

David was shocked. "You can talk!"

Smiling Ade the Lion, nodded. "Yes I can. But you must listen to me. Playing Mums and Dads are not for children to play. Now go and shout to all the children that showed you that game 'I said no' and a magical thing will happen."

"What? What will happen?" asked David.

Ade said, "You will be able to create a new game for children to play."

"Thank you so much Lion," said David. Ade roared he knew his mission was done.

The Game Doctors & Nurses: children playing
A doctor and a nurse where looking at bodies can be involved.

Mission: Aba the Monkey
Young person: 9-year-old Lisa

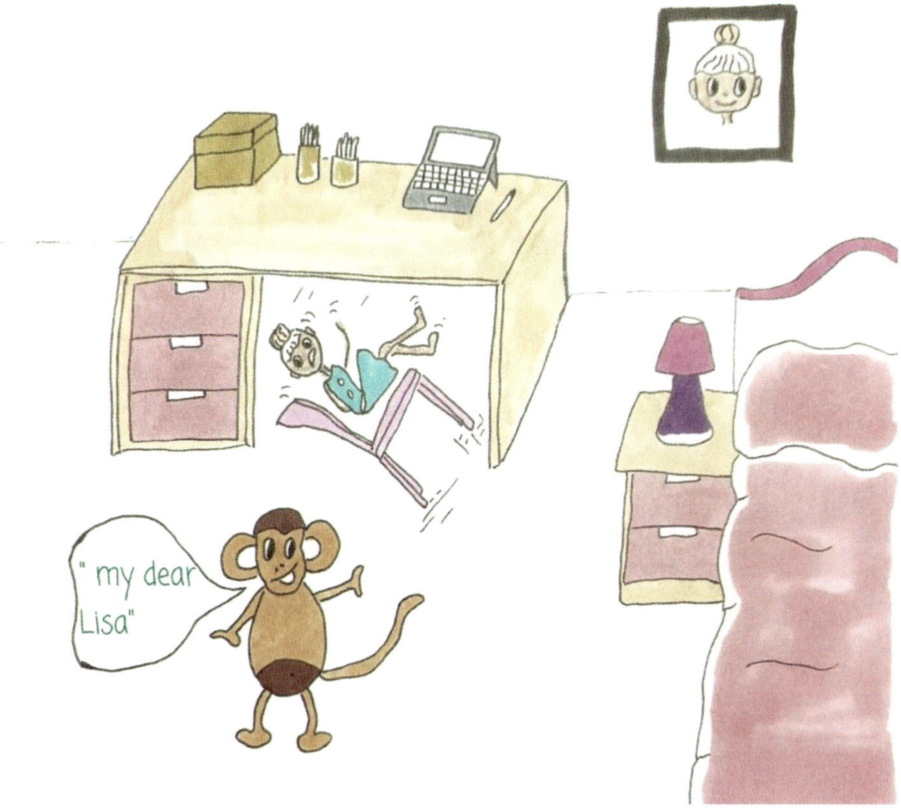
" my dear Lisa"

Lisa had one brother and two sisters and they all loved playing together, having fun. One day Lisa shared a game called Doctors and Nurses.

This was Aba's chance to get into the room and speak to Lisa.

"My dear Lisa," Aba said.

Shocked, Lisa nearly fell off a chair she was sitting on, in her room. "How did you get in here and you can talk?"

"Yes I can," Aba smiled. "I've come to give you a message. Doctors and Nurses and touching other children's private parts is not a game for children. Now when you go back to the children that showed you that game, shout: 'I said No!' That game is not for children. Then watch, a magical thing will happen."

"What will that be?" asked Lisa.

"You will have the power to create another a safer game to play."

Lisa was overjoyed. "Wow that sounds like fun, thank you so much monkey."

"I'll let you into something else too," said Aba. "When you are older, you *will* become a doctor."

Lisa was stunned with excitement; she could not say anything.

Aba did a somersault. She was pleased she had finished her mission.

The Game Girlfriends & Boyfriends: children
Playing a girlfriend and boyfriend.

Mission: Asha, the Elephant
Young person: 10-year-old Ken

Youth Club
Let's play boyfriends and girlfriends
What is that big thing.

Ken loved going to his youth club. It was there that the young people did a lot of activities. Even so, they were still bored. So, his friends came up with a game called Boyfriends and Girlfriends that they could play. Ken did not want to play but did not know how to say no.

Asha, the Elephant sat outside the youth club, waiting, she knew this was her chance to step in. This was when Ken saw her.

"What is that big thing over there?" Ken asked as he went over.

"I'm here to help you have a voice," said Asha, the Elephant.

"Wow! You can talk!" exclaimed Ken excitedly.

Asha laughed. "Yes I can. I can also see that you don't want to play that game and don't know how to say no."

Taking her trunk, she places it on his head. "Now when you go back you will shout: "I said NO!" And magic will happen."

"What magic?" asked Ken, looking very excited.

"You'll have the power to create another game to play that they will play with you."

Ken headed off, shouting, "Thank you so much elephant."

Turning her trunk high above her head Asha proudly walked off. She had made a difference to a child's life.

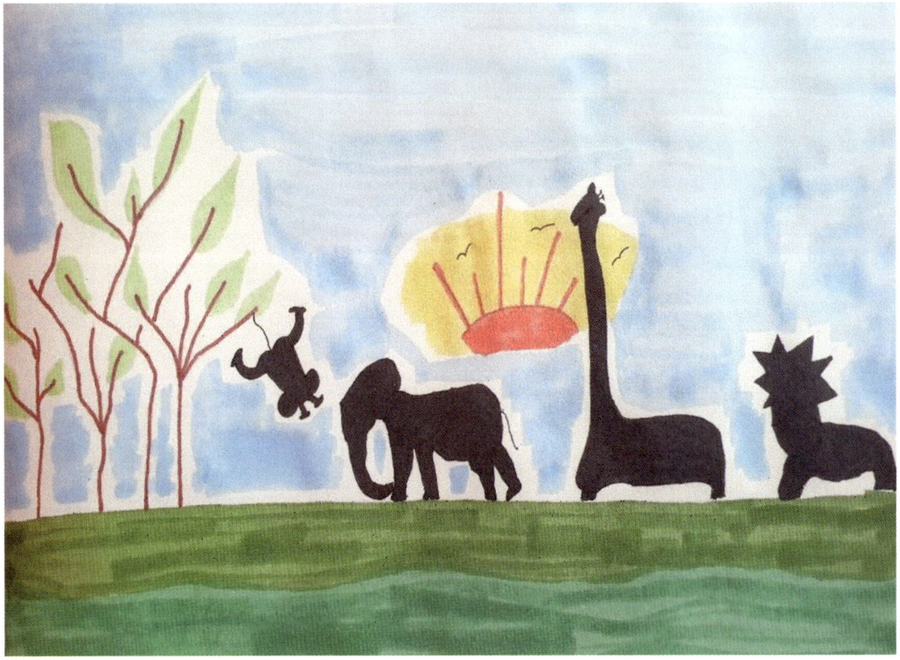

Their mission has finished, the animals got back together to share their stories about the children they had met.

Aba said, "Yes we did it now let the real magic begin…"

The animals made their way back home to Kenya in Africa.

THE END

Pronunciation of the African names:
Kwame= Kw-a-me
Aba= A-ba
Asha= A-sha
Ade= A-dee
Fumi= Fu-me

About the Author:

Zoe Pennant is a foster carer, educational psychologist and youth coach who has worked with children and young people for over 15 years. Her experiences in this subject about children's body safety, personal boundaries and knowing when to say no, has led her to write this children's book.

This book can be used in training workshops, staff training and in the home. A way to breakdown a subject that adults still find uncomfortable to talk about. May it help to break the silence for both children and adults who have a fear of speaking out about child-on-child sexual abuse.

Printed in Great Britain
by Amazon